EAST OF
LOS ANGELES

John Brantingham

Anaphora Literary Press

Anna Faktorovich: Director, Designer, Editor

104 Banff Dr., Apt. 101, Edinboro, PA 16412

(814) 273-0004

pennsylvaniajournal@gmail.com

www.anaphoraliterary.wordpress.com

Published in 2011 by Anaphora Literary Press

East of Los Angeles

John Brantingham—1st edition.

ISBN-13: 978-1-460-92520-1

ISBN-10: 1-460-92520-3

Library of Congress Control Number: 2011902602

For Annie

ACKNOWLEDGEMENTS

"A Blessing" was published in *Askew*; "Putting in a Window" and "When I Call" were read by Garrison Keillor on *Writer's Almanac* and originally were published in my chapbook *Putting in a Window,* Finishing Line Press, with "The First Signs of Spring" and "Just before the Fire"; "At the End of the Day" was published in *The New Laurel Review*; "Home Tectonics" was published in *Earthshine*; "We Turn out the Lights" and "Los Angeles" were published in *Freefall*; "Ah, That the World Could Be L.A." was published in *Iota*; "The Art of Falling" was published in *Borderlines*; "There'd better be someone dead up there," "You Are," and "The natural history of the world," were all published by *Atlantic Pacific Press*; "Morning Rituals" was published by *Pearl Magazine*; "Let's Hope We Fit in" and "A Garden Caught in Amber" were published in *Mediterranean Garden,* Finishing Line Press; "How I Felt" was published in *The Chiron Review* (before I was an editor there); and "Icarus Lives" was published in *Heroes for Today,* Pudding House Press.

TABLE OF CONTENTS

I

II

III

IV

A Blessing

In the backyard, the Oldsmobile
that hasn't started in three months
has become a table for men.
They pour Cutty Sark over ice
in day glo plastic cups and talk
car repair. I'm there too, eight years old
and almost completely deaf, hiding

from the sun, under the car
and licking my hand for its salt.
Their muffled speech comes
to me "ronronron" as though
they're chanting a prayer to Ron,
the god of auto repair. When I'm
bored with my hand, I turn to watch

their shuffling feet until their chant
brings me peace, and the salt
on my tongue, the valley heat,
the smell of whiskey and cigarettes,
the browning grass beneath me,
and Ron's soothing blessing
helps me to drift off to sleep.

L.A. Is Burning Again

and when
the freeway *rushes*
arcs

close
to a grass
fire, *) dying*

the heat
creeps
into

my Saturn,
and sears← 1   ← *sadness*
my right cheek.

look up

It's Just Me Here

I'm nine and staring into the dark green
water at the arboretum. Catfish
flit along the edge of the pond coming

into my field of vision just
for a moment before they disappear.
Looking across the expanse of the lake,

I feel like they're doing a dance down there
or they're part of some great pattern, and I'm
seeing only the tiniest part of it.

It's like I'm on the edge of understanding,
of seeing the design. It's the same
above me. Crows, in groups and alone,

have been traveling South East all morning,
and they clearly have a purpose—they're
going someplace specific on some grand

mission of a magnitude that requires
the entire crow nation, and I think
that if I could just get a different angle

on either of them, the catfish or the crows,
if I could gain some perspective, I could
comprehend all of it, that I would have

the answer to every mystery, but it's
just me here, standing off to the side
of the lawn, a little bit away from my family,

staring at the edge of the lake and a corner
of the sky, trying to understand it all
by watching the little I can see.

L.A. in the Late Afternoon

It's 1978, and I'm sitting cross-legged
in the bushes in the front yard secretly
watching my dad mow the lawn.
The smog is coming in thick waves like fog,
and Dad goes around back and forth moving
slowly to the left cutting the grass, and choking
in the heat. I lost most of my hearing
a week ago, so I can't hear him cough
or the lawn mower or the cars driving by
or the wind in the bush where I'm hiding.
What I do hear is the last thing he told me
about before I went deaf. He told about
how my grandfather made it through
the great depression as a milk man,
the old kind with a horse drawn carriage.
My grandfather died before I was born,
so when I think of him, I imagine that
he looks like Dad. It's an odd moment
—my dad is in front of me, but my grandfather
is too, and though I don't know it,
my great grandfather and his father
and a line of men ahead of them reaching
to who knows when, all of them there
in front of me, puffing their way
through the late afternoon smog.

Continuation?

Maybe If I Squint

It's 1978, and I lost my hearing a few months ago.
We're cruising down the ten freeway at noon,
and I know we're going on a trip, but I don't

know where because no one has told me.
The light coming through the window warms
my skin almost to sweating, and the car

rocks me gently. The hubcaps of the cars
passing by are swirling designs and seem
to run backwards. I close my eyes and am

plunged into a warm oblivion. I might
as well be surrounded by amniotic fluid. ck
Later, when I'm bounced awake, we're

outside of Los Angeles somewhere surrounded
by fields of lemon trees. I want to close my eyes
again and go back to that place, but my mother

has turned to me and is saying something
and pointing out the window, so I stare
into the rows of trunks and try to see what she sees.

lost hearing / good sense / vival of other senses

Music from Another Room

The Los Angeles of my youth was a silent place,
but, of course, everywhere was silent for me then.
I would lose my hearing for months at a time

and was stuck in this world without anyone,
completely cut off. When I'd lose my hearing,
I'd descend into a sort of trance created

by months without a single conversation
and this whooshing following me around
all the time. It was a trance filled with novels

that would blend with the day dreams
created by boiling Santa Ana winds and were
more real than the mute images around me until I

couldn't tell the difference between fantasy
and reality, until they blended together. Now,
I don't ever want to go back to that world,

but sometimes with the war and the vulgar evil
my students have to live through and traffic
and all the rest—right on down to the war—

a world where bears dance to a music
only I can hear, seems like a reasonable
trade for friendship, a career and even jazz.

What I Remember

It takes a while before you realize
that the vast desert, this great expanse
of death, isn't quiet. You start out
by hearing the wind that's always going,
and then you pick up the little things
like coyotes and snakes and even mice.
You start to come out here more,
and you see that there are as many kinds
of desert as there are ways to die,
and it's peaceful, but not empty. The scrub
starts to become like a friend and the sand
does too, and the animals are mellow
enough if you just watch them. After
a while, you come in out of the city
just for the afternoon, and you think
to yourself that this wouldn't be such
a bad place to spend an eternity after all.

[handwritten annotations in right margin: "Can't hear right?", "imagining like?"]

Putting in a Window

Carpentry has a rhythm that should never
be violated. You need to move slowly,
methodically, never trying to finish early,
never even hoping that you'd be done sooner.
It's best if you work without thought of the end.
If hurried, you end up with crooked
door joints and drafty rooms. Do not work
after you are annoyed just so the job
will be done more quickly. Stop when you
begin to curse at the wood. Putting in
a window should be a joy. You should love
the new header and the sound of
your electric screwdriver as it secures
the new beams. The only good carpenter
is the one who knows that he's not good.
He's afraid that he'll ruin the whole house,
and he works slowly. It's the same as
cooking or driving. The good cook
knows humility, and his soufflé never falls
because he is terrified that it will fall
the whole time he's cooking. The good driver
knows that he might plow into a mother
walking her three-year old, and so watches
for them carefully. The good carpenter
knows that his beams might be weak, and a misstep
might ruin the place he loves. In the end,
you find your own pace, and you lose time.
When you started, the sun was high and now
that you're finished, it's dark. Tomorrow, you

might put in a door. The next day,
you'll start on your new deck.

main idea?

The First Signs of Spring

The first signs of spring this year are larvae.
They come out of the pines on long invisible
web strings. The wind catches them and swirls
them about, so hundreds of floating
yellow/green worms fill the air. Every time
I walk outside, a half dozen larvae
float out of nowhere and smack me in the face
or drop on my head and get tangled   ← funny
in my hair. There's no stopping them or keeping
them out of the house. Larvae fall into
the grocery bags and into a glass of water.
Larvae get into the house and my dog's fur.
When I smack them on my clothes, I get
the most beautiful yellow/green splotches
on my nice white shirts. In the morning,
I wake up with one crawling across
my left cheek and another on my arm.
The rest of the day all I can think about
is one crawling into my head
and every time my hair brushes my lobe,
③→ I spasmodically thrust my little finger
down my ear hole to keep the little bastards
from setting up house-keeping. I do this
little maneuver one too many times
during class in the morning, and I yell
"Damn it" as I do it, and my eighteen-
year olds look at each other quizzically   have has
and at me with a little bit of fear.
I almost explain myself but then think

better of it. The second sign of spring
is that I feel dangerous.   Let them think
that I am a sociopath. Let them think I'm
fighting internal demons. Better they think
that than know I'm scratching invisible worms.

In the Late Afternoon

Rick sticks his head over the wall
to point out that I'm giving
the lavender too much water.

I generally listen to his
advice about the garden. He
grows tomatoes as juicy as

cacti and oranges too and since
the diagnosis, marijuana
that comes in thick and unstoppable,

and I take it for granted that
he has a green thumb. It's in the late
afternoon that I can smell him

in the backyard using it, blocking
whatever pain he can, and it
puts him in a contemplative

frame of mind. What he generally
contemplates are gardens, mine and his,
and who knows, maybe his other

neighbor's too. Sometimes, he comes
over after he's done, to bullshit
I guess, and sit in my Adirondack

chair and stretch his bare feet out
into the lippia and let the cool
leaves find their way between his toes.

Tuesday Yellow

The first cold day in fall,
and everything is yellow.
The woods are yellow,
the sky is yellow,
my mood is yellow.
I don't know if having
a yellow mood is good
or not, but out here, I'm
finally alone enough to feel it.

Watch Out

This morning,
Garrison Keillor
read my poem
on Writer's Almanac.
I looked through
the online archive
to find that
yesterday he read
one by Shakespeare,
and in a couple
of days, it's going
to be Sharon Olds.
Now, if my friends
and colleagues
thought it was
just about impossible
to talk to me before,
they have no idea
what an insufferable ass
I plan to be
from now on.

At the End of the Day

By the time we come up over the hill,
everyone is asleep in the van. This is
a far corner of the Mojave that I drive
through every night, and every night
the train is parked on its tracks pointed
right at me, waiting before it makes
its way out, and every night when I come
over the hill, I flash my brights. I don't
know what I'm hoping for. Maybe I hope
he'll blast the horn or flash his lights back,
but he never does. The road brings the van
along the side of the train, and it's only
a hundred feet between the conductor and me.
I can see him through his window, sitting there
staring out into the infinite darkness, populating
some world in his head. It's just a slice of desert
between the two of us and if he would look
through his window, he would see my eyes
and I would see his, but he never does.
Tonight, I'll drive another forty-five minutes—
first through scrub and then up into the forest—
and he'll push his train out to who knows
where, and we'll both watch the darkness
in front of us, and it would have been so easy
for him to turn his head and forget that he's alone,
but he didn't, and I don't think that he ever will.

Home Tectonics

Our house is at the crest
of a mountain formed
by a fault line that's still
doing its work. We're up
over five thousand feet,
and probably, slowly, the spot

that we sit on is going
to get higher and higher.
So at some point, the house
is coming down, shaken
to bits, I suppose, and what
we're banking on is that
we've chosen the right moment

in geologic time, a sweet
spot between cataclysms.
And that's what Annie and I
hope for generally,
and what everyone seems
to want—some forgettable

moment between great wars
or typhoons or plagues—to have
timed it just right, so we're
in just the right place between
what we read about in history
books and the moments after
which history won't matter much.

Just Before the Fire

We're the last people
on our block during
the voluntary

evacuation, and
I walk the street. The
houses are quiet. The

yards are quiet. The
cars are quiet. It's
how I picture Christmas

Eve when I hear the
old carols, and I want
to stay here forever.

When You're Caught by Surprise

It's surprising when you finally reach
the age when you see changes in your town.
The mall has gone from being twenty-three
little shops to two megastores and an office
supply place, and there are houses that used
to be the vacant lot the kids took over.
At the back of your mind, you always knew
this would happen, but you never expected
that the mountain would change too. It seemed
permanent, not the trees, the forest. Last year's
fire changed even geology, sending
giant boulders tumbling off into canyons.
The deep snow of winter gouged your favorite
streambed, making it maybe three feet deeper.
Someone, a hundred or more years ago,
put up some barbed wire to fence in cattle.
After the wooden posts collapsed, the wire was
covered by debris that turned into earth.
The wire has been down in the mountain
festering like a splinter for who knows how long.
This year the ground has finally worked it out.
On your daily walk, it catches your foot.
It makes you feel so damn old to see
the mountain changing, and that makes you think
about yourself and how much you've changed,
and you wonder what the fifteen year old
you once were would think of you today.

Monday Morning in Late October

The fog comes in over night and cuts us
off, and by the time Archie drags me out
the front door for his walk, everything is
dark and quiet except for the sound of fog
water dripping off the leaves and my footsteps
and Archie's footsteps. Later today, I'll
have to come down off the mountain and drive
into LA to go to work and deal
with traffic and students and the city
and everything that goes along with it,
but something about the rhythm of the dripping
and the footsteps and the smell that fog has
after it's been filtered through pine makes me
think that maybe there's nothing down there
below us, no cars, no guns, no drugs, no
AA, no history, no future, none
of that, and no need for any of it
either, and maybe LA's just some distant
memory. It feels like there's just the two
of us and my little house with my wife
and the other dog up here in the trees
or that if we wanted we could just put up
our own flag and declare our own country
and be done with the rest of the world,
but it doesn't take long for the walk
to be done, and it takes only a little
longer for the fog to burn off, and pretty
soon after that I find myself bouncing

along in the truck towards all of it, the whole
stew, and I figure out that what I'm thinking
about isn't the mess but my students
and my friends who teach with me, and it occurs
to me that LA's not such a bad place to be.

We Turn Out the Lights

Annie and I like to turn out the porch lights
and watch the satellites fly by. Up here in the
mountains so much is beautiful. The city below
is peaceful, calm, twinkling, dressed up like
Christmas or the party of some little girl's
imagination. It's only at some distorted
middle length that satellites look like space
trash and a city falls into cliché, torn apart
and dangerous. Far away they sparkle, and
close up you see the precision of mechanics
or a single person just doing what he can
to help his friends make it to the next day.

Ah, That the World Could Be L.A.

Instead of taking roll every morning,
I ask my students a question of the day,
and this morning's question is what

other time period would they have liked
to have lived in. It's a fairly banal question,
but they have fun with it, especially

a group of four friends sitting in the back
who all say they wished they could be
a part of the Crusades. When it's Sepehr's

turn, my one Persian student, he turns
to them and in a fist shaking parody
of what we see presented in movies

and on television, he says "I would
like to live during the Crusades too."
This is the Los Angeles I'm so in love with.

The ones sitting in the back were serious
about wanting to Crusade, and maybe
Sepehr's answer was only half joking,

but the Middle East is the Middle East,
and it's as far away as it could be,
and they all like Sepehr, and in fact

in the class, Ben, a conservative Jew is
Sepehr's closest friend, and the two leave
the classroom later talking about their

weekend plans. Perhaps, LA is as vanilla
and plastic as the world says it is,
and maybe out here we've lost touch

with the traditional values of the East,
but in the end, I believe I'd take this peace
over that kind of authenticity every single time.

She Thinks She's Looking at Venus

when the red light
on the plane's
wing flashes

as it comes
in on approach
to LAX,

but she decides
that it doesn't have
to be a planet to be pretty,

and she watches
her Venus come down
to touch the Earth.

Stanley's on the Freeway When He Gets the Call

that his wife has given birth
to a girl, and although
it doesn't make sense,

he starts to laugh out loud.
He laughs and laughs,
can't stop himself,

doesn't want to—
laughs so hard in fact
that people in nearby cars

can hear him, and his joy creeps
into their bones, and despite
their daily pain, they laugh too.

The Art of Falling

On the freeway overpasses,
on a motorcycle,
you sit four feet off the ground,

and the guardrails are two feet high,
and when traffic is moving,
you lean into those turns,

the way that you lean into any turn,
falling towards the ground a bit to keep
yourself up right, pushing yourself despite yourself

towards the void between you
and the people below who could be
your final breathless audience.

It's Eight in the Morning When the Freeway Comes to a Dead Stop

Gary looks to his left
to see Rob, his best friend
from high school,

gone pink from yelling
at the traffic
that's not going to move.

He's sure it's Rob,
and sure
that in twenty years,

this is
the Rob
that he'll remember.

A Sentimental Poem About Los Angeles

In the morning during
L.A.'s June Gloom,
if you overlook the low clouds,

you can trace the freeways.
The heat of all those cars
with all those people

rushing off to do jobs
they don't want to do
for people they love

cuts through
the murk above
and around them.

Another Sentimental Poem
About Los Angeles

What I missed most
when I moved away
to the mountains

for five years
was the hopeful rumble
of the 10 freeway.

Now that I live
a hundred yards from it,
I leave my windows open

to be lulled asleep
by the sound of people
going where they'd rather be.

A Less Than Sentimental Poem About Los Angeles

A man changing his tire
on the side of the freeway lurches /9
forward as he strips the lug nut.

He knows that he's not going
to get the tire off by himself,
knows he's going

to miss his meeting,
knows he's going to be fired,
knows his cell phone's not charged,

and he knows for certain that he'll
try to wave people over,
but no one's going to stop.

Gary Wakes Up on the 110 Freeway

He's in the passenger seat
—his brother is driving—
just as they pass

under a bridge
designed to look
modern in 1920.

Considering its arch,
its lines, and the echo
the tires make as

they pass through,
he is once and finally
entirely in the moment.

He Immigrated to L.A. as a Child

After they got off the plane, his father had packed
them into a van. On the freeway, he had been
silenced by the reflectors.

Here, he had thought, they were
so rich they put lights
on the roads. He hadn't lost that

feeling when he was told
the truth. He even has it now,
coming over the rise,

seeing the reflectors
and the entire Los Angeles night
spread out before him.

Your Favorite Jazz Radio Station

Even way out where no one lives,
you can hear talk radio—mostly
people saying the same things
your least favorite uncle tells
you after a couple of drinks.

Closer to the perimeter,
country music, news radio
and oldies stations help to keep
you awake. You dream about sitting
in the back seat, listening

to your parents arguments,
and driving to Mt. Rushmore.
Then come classic rock, alternative
rock and classical music
at about the same place

in the suburbs with fights
in minivans between the generations.
But when you get far enough
in the city that corruption
and brutality is painted

on the walls near the freeway,
you can always find a jazz station,
not at the physical center,
but somewhere a little to the left,
where the real city moved

when the downtown apartment
buildings were torn down
and replaced with warehouses,
museums, bus depots, train stations,
giant office buildings

that you're not supposed to go into,
parking garages, and overpasses.
It moved with the people
who scrub the office buildings
and spend long days in little booths

just inside the parking structures.
They work the warehouses
and guard the museums.
The communists in town
were born there or moved there

for a couple of years after college.
Most of the people who can hear
your favorite jazz radio station,
don't listen to it. The communists
have too much revolution to think about,

the kid who works the parking booth
listens to the Morning Zoo on K-Something,
and the people who are allowed
into the office building dream
of news reports from Wall Street.

Only four people you know actually listen
to jazz radio, and you know for a fact that
each one of them, without exception,
gets up every morning and says,
"God, I love this city."

Los Angeles

My love for you, King Smog,
is the love of an old woman
for an old man. I love you with all
of your faults, even sometimes because
of your faults. I love your freeways,
your 5, 405, 605, 105—
your 10, 210, 110, 710
and for your pesticide beaches
choked with human waste too dangerous
to bathe in but too beautiful
not to. I love you for your LACMA
and MOCA and Getty and your free
jazz concerts and your expensive
jazz concerts. I love you even
when your hills burn orange sherbet,
and when you quake your buildings down,
and when murderous hot winds come
just when I thought the summer heat
was gone. I love you for torrential
rains and mudslides and strip malls
and romances. I love you
when your air creeps in on little
cat claws, climbing onto my chest,
choking me with methane breath.
I love you for your insane Friday
afternoons—everyone on a mission
somewhere and no one moving anywhere.
I love you for Claremont, Santa
Monica, Beverly Hills, Northridge,

and Long Beach, even when
Long Beach Harbor smells
of dirty dish rags three days gone.
And even though I've said
I will leave you, Lord Smog,
the first chance I have, I think
I'll stay with you until they scatter
my ashes on Pacific Coast Highway,
and the desert winds blow me
into the infinity of your endless suburbs.

Geriatrics

It doesn't take long for people to get old.
Mostly it happens in an afternoon
or maybe one early morning.

The man who comes home earlier
than his wife thought he would
goes back to work bitter and defeated.

The woman who ran 5K races
slips in the shower
and is finally 87 years old,

and the girl who went in for surgery
that didn't go right, won't be young again
until much, much later.

In a Canadian School

On my first day of giving readings
in Canada, they have me come
into a school and talk to some
students about poetry, and they're

kids, so when I ask them if they
have any questions, they don't ask
about Dylan Thomas but about
Los Angeles, which is where I'm from.

They ask me if I've been
to Disneyland, and I tell them
that my wife used to work there,
which is true. They ask me if I

know any celebrities, and I
tell them that I jog with Wesley
Snipes and play poker with Quentin
Tarantino, which is not true,

but I want to give them their money's
worth, and they're agog with the idea
of palm trees and beaches
and earthquakes and the people they see

on television. It's the first
nice day of spring, so we're doing
this outside—the pine trees ahead
of me and the lake behind—

when I notice above me one
of those V formations that I've
always heard of, thirty maybe
fifty geese. Having lived my life

in California, I have, of course,
read about this, and I think I've seen
a goose in a movie once, but it's
something else to watch them in person.

It's been like this all week, new moments
that I've dreamed of, an iced lake,
the clean smell of Canada, the trees,
the lakes, rivers, and fish. I've even

seen a porcupine, but when I ask them
about the geese, their young eyes
have already become cynical
with the routine. They tell me

about the birds, but they want
to get back to L.A. They're lost,
completely gone, in their dreams
of Los Angeles, and here I am

dreaming my northern dreams,
none of us fantasizing
about what we have, none of us
seeing what's really there.

The Blair Witch Project

I woke up this morning thinking about a student
who was in my class—I don't know—
ten or more years ago. He'd seen *The Blair Witch Project*
and declared that it had changed his life.
He'd taken the stance that it really was real,
that there was a witch and those kids had actually died,
all of it had happened no matter who in the classroom
made fun of him. He said that after this movie,
nothing else in his life could ever be the same,
and he was serious about that.
I woke up this morning, feeling a little sorry for him,
and wondering whether or not he still remembers
the film that did so much for him at the time.
I wondered whether he could ever
have another moment like that again,
completely lost in that fantasy or whether, he has become
just like the all of those people who mocked him,
that day. They'd universally adopted the false wisdom
of cynicism, but only because their own fantasies had
already failed them so completely.

IV

Morning Rituals

The house is always peaceful in the mornings.
At breakfast, Annie and I talk about
little things like the food we're eating, or we
make jokes with the dog. After breakfast,
Annie puts on her make-up. This is ritual
—always the same. She puts on the base first,
spreading it evenly, not with fingertips
but the whole first segments of three fingers
—the parts opposite the nails. Then the lipstick,
which she doesn't put on the way movie stars
do. She rubs the red into her right index
finger and then pulls it across her lips. She
uses only a little mascara, and
she doesn't open her mouth when she strokes her
lashes, which is the way I've seen all other
women do it. Our bedroom is very
warm. We talk about little things while she
does her make-up, like what we'll do on the weekend
or we just joke around with the dog.

Let's Hope We Fit In

In our front yard, we have a pomegranate tree
sitting there waiting for Persephone's return
in Spring, and in the back there's a bay tree
for any Olympian from the classical
age of Greece who might happen by. We have
an olive tree too, and I don't know the myth
about that one, but one of those Greeks must have
been into olives. Anyway, Annie and I seem
to be preparing for a return to some age
of heroes and gods, and I don't know if they'll
be bothered by the ten freeway running
nearly through our yard, or the rap music
thumping down the streets or the planes
taking off from Ontario Airport or the buses,
the smog, the dogs barking at kids high on whatever,
the strip malls or the concrete rivers,
but Annie and I are just fine.

When I Call

As I talk to her,
I like to think of
our paperback copy
of Thomas More's
Utopia sitting

on the phone table.
No one reads *Utopia*.
No one has ever
read *Utopia*.
No one has ever

wanted to read
Utopia, not
even Thomas More.
The only action
it will ever see

is when she absently
flips its pages while
she talks to me. When
I call, I like to
think of her doing that.

Los Angeles, June 22, 2007

I admit that I enjoy sitting
in the backyard sipping some drink
and dreaming of Rome during the reign
of Augustus or of Athens back when
the world was the Mediterranean,

and I'm even guilty of reading
about the American revolution
and watching bad movies about Camelot.
I believe that I would have liked
to see the Jazz Age or the Restoration

of Charles II or even the late 1940s,
and I suppose that the world
might improve in the future,
but this afternoon, my wife and I
—plebeians by anyone's standard—

saw the Space Shuttle up above
the San Gabriel Mountains as we
drove into the Norton Simon
Museum of Art to see the world's
premier Jawlensky exhibit,

and we heard the sonic boom playing
a brief counterpoint to the history's
best jazz station, and I was forced
to give up my illusions about wanting
to live in some romantic and glorious age.

I'll take LA, my friends, over Camelot,
Atlantis, and even El Dorado. I'll
take LA over Swinging London,
even if they introduced me to John Lennon
even if they let me star in *Blow Up*.

You Are

Darling, you know
you are like one of those
marble statues
in the British Museum,

one of those they put out
for students and tourists to prove
that the English
know perfection,

one of those they stole
from the Greeks
and can't bear
to give back,

or one of those they stole
from the sea floor and the sunfish
who used to worship
them in a watery way,

one of those they stole
because the Greeks made form sing
and reminded each other
of how good good could be,

so good that whole civilizations
are suggested in the curving line
on some forgotten goddess's smiling lip.

Darling, you know you are
that beautiful,
so it's with love
that I say you have a big nose,

and last night as we kissed, you inhaled
and pulled me inside of you,
down into your lungs, and I swam around
in your warm blood until it drowsed me.

I swam downstream looking for a place
to rest and found your stomach,
where a pillow of baklava
lay waiting for me,

and when I drifted off to sleep,
I dreamed of you,
of your muscles, tissues,
bones, and bowels,

each part perfect enough to suggest
an entire civilization,
and I dreamed that you were my goddess,
and I was your willing sunfish.

I swam around you and worshipped
you for millennia as the British drifted by
in ships above, stealing and stealing,
but missing us down here
in the perfect temple of the sea.

The Natural History of the World

is written on your body,
millions of years, millions and millions.
Your forebear was a fish, a beast
who roamed the depths spending his days
trying not to die in the cold dark waters
that heaved relentlessly around him,
and you take after him.
You have his flashing eyes,
his sleekness, his pulsing endless life.
Surrounding you is his ridiculous hope,
the hope that kept him moving,
dodging the monsters that lived there,
the vitality that attracted his watery wife to him,
the faith that he gave to his children
who passed it on to theirs
who had the good sense (after a while)
to stand up and walk out of that tomb.
You have his energy and passion,
and in your eyes, I can see him
joyful, playful, and beautiful.

Hot House

God, it was hot in the house last night.
You'd been cooking that casserole in the oven,
and I had the rice going on the range,
and the dishes were washing and the clothes
were drying and the computer was printing out
my entire novel, and all of that got me burning
into a sweat that I just couldn't stop. It got to me,
so I took a deep breath, one that filled my lungs
and beyond, one that got into my chest,
down in my stomach, seeped in my arms and legs,
and even into my brain until I was fat on
that hot oxygen, and when I stepped out
into the cool evening air, I began to float.

I got up into the breezes, up over L.A., up where
I could cool down a bit, and when I did,
I let the air seep out, little by little, and I sank back
down towards you. Up there, my love,
I could have seen it all. I could have seen all the way
to Anaheim and the fireworks over Disneyland
and Long Beach harbor its magnificent Queen Mary.
I could have seen all those wonderful loafers loafing
on Catalina, but what do I want to look out there for,
when right where I was, right down there framed
by my instep was all that warmth, all the quiet hum
of cleaning, cooking, and printing, with that perfect
smell
of eggplant casserole, and you, wondering where I'd
gone.

Just Outside of Los Angeles

It's nearly midnight, and Gary's backyard is dark,
and the police must be chasing someone because
the helicopter's spotlight turns it all into day.

That giant white light shows him everything,
his wife's plants, the kids' toys, his brother's dead car.
It's nearly midnight, and Gary's backyard was dark

but he sees it all now, and it seems that he never
noticed how little of him was there before
the helicopter's spotlight turned it all into day.

This life is his wife's, his kids', his brother's
and he, what is he? An afterthought? The cash?
It's nearly midnight, and Gary's backyard is dark

again, and his groping hand finds his wife's tree,
and without thinking, he plucks a pomegranate.
The helicopter's spotlight turns it all into day

once more, and he sees the fruit in his hand, that
perfect red fruit, and he brings it to his nose to inhale.
It's nearly midnight, and Gary's backyard is dark, but
the helicopter's spotlight has turned it all into day.

Flipping Through the Cable Stations at 3:27am, I Stop at the NASA Channel

With all that's out there, the black holes,
new suns, planets, worlds, comets,
and well you know, they turn the cameras
back towards Earth, so we can watch

cloud formations and shorelines
that are indistinguishable from 100 miles up.
All of the lands begin to look like one,
and sitting here, I might be watching

my beautiful LA or Cairo—it doesn't matter.
It's funny, all of those billions of dollars,
and we just want another view of ourselves.
After all, a nebula floating out in space is just gas
/2.

that probably dissipated millennia ago,
and it might be pretty, but there is no love out there.
Only Earth has love, and it's healthy
to pull the cameras back and watch the mess

from this kind of distance, to get some perspective
before I go back to sleep only to wake up tomorrow
and go back into it all trying to remember love
when I'm not 100 miles up.

How I Felt

There was one time in the dead
center of summer after we'd
had a Santa Ana, and the glass
on the windows seemed ready
to melt but the Santa Ana was over
and storm clouds had moved in. A snap
of lightning and all the rain in the world
landed on our street. It poured for three
minutes and moved on. When it was gone,
the street steamed and hissed
until it was dry again. Last night,
I woke up at two in the morning.
You were lying perfectly still,
and you didn't know I was watching you.
When I saw you lying there so quietly last night,
that's just exactly how I felt.

A Garden Caught in Amber

Sometimes after midnight, I meet myself out
in the garden, the me of twenty-five years ago.
We get along pretty well as long as I'm willing
to play catch or some hiding game until another
me shows up, a little older or younger, but hair

still not gray and still no paunch. It doesn't take
long before we're all there tromping through
the lavender, cutting ourselves on succulents
or eating raw squash. The eighty-year-old me
watches the throng with his quiet solemnity,

not (the rest of us hope) judging too harshly
until it's time for them to go in, and they
file out one by one leaving me there alone.
I'm always the last to go in because I like
the garden more than the rest of them.

For the old folks, it's passe and the kids are
interested in girls or rifles or whatever,
but I could sit out there in the cold all night,
squinting at the flowers and trying to see
their ghost images in the reflected amber city lights.

You Gotta Be Careful

The first time I saw Daedalus was down
at Acres of Books in Long Beach.
I told him that I just regained my hearing
after a pretty long period of deafness
that left me reading everything I could
because no one could talk to me.
Daedalus nodded, smiled distantly,
and said, "You gotta be careful though.
Reading's fine. Reading's great,

but it's not everything." He rubbed
his stubble, three days gone. "I mean
look at me. I was your typical bookworm
as a kid. I never fit in, so I was always
reading. I got to be the brightest kid
in the kingdom, and that paid off,
but I never learned to deal with people,
to be with people. If I could have
learned to talk to people, Icarus

probably would..." He couldn't
find a way to say it, and his face
twisted up in wrinkles of suffering, so I told
him I understood. I did too. I really did.
I wondered what he was like in the old days
before Icarus fell to his death,
but I suppose as technically brilliant
as he had been, he didn't become
a genius until he learned about pain.

Down by the Pier

I saw Daedalus one time when I was
jogging along the coast in Seal Beach.
He was down by the breakers by himself
staring out over the water. I'd heard
that back in the early days after
Icarus had fallen to his death he'd
bounced around the Greek islands on
the off chance his son had turned his fall
into a dive and had lived through it,
but he wasn't doing that now. I thought
about going down and talking to him
and giving him whatever comfort I
could, but I knew it was a bad idea.
Sometimes, we're just alone, and no one
can be there for us, and as painful as that
is, being taken away from it is much worse.

Flying Too Low

The last time I saw Daedalus, he was
down near Dodger Stadium in some dive
bar drinking alone. I sat down next to him,
I'm ashamed to say, not because he was
alone, but because he was a star,
the one famous person I knew, and I
was with friends. He talked about Icarus
again, always Icarus, and I fed
him some platitude about moving on,
and he nodded, his eyes staring at something
miles away through the barroom wall until
I left him alone telling myself I
didn't know his brand of pain. They found him
hanging by his neck from one of the Os
in the Hollywood sign a week after that.
He didn't leave a note, but he must
have known that we wouldn't need one.

Icarus Lives

Sure, the wax melted, and he fell,
but his father never came
back to check up on him. Icarus
turned the fall into a dive,
and although he had the wind knocked
out of him, he was able to float
on his back until he was picked up
by a steamer headed to LA.
LA seemed the perfect place for him
at first. He thought he'd capitalize
on his fame, maybe get someone
to ghost write a book for him
and then hit up all the talk shows,
but what he found outside of the hustle
of downtown was a kind of peace
in the suburbs. The weather was nice
in Huntington Beach, and if he let his father
think he was dead, he could avoid any
further hair-brained schemes involving
minotaurs. He unloads real estate now
and has a couple of kids of his own.
The trick, he says in his Hawaiian shirt
at a block party, isn't in telling your kids
not to fly too high, but knowing
when they're old enough for wings.

OTHER ANAPHORA LITERARY PRESS TITLES

British Literature
Pennsylvania Literary Journal
Summer 2010
Edited by: Anna Faktorovich
1-4563-0432-1; paperback; 208 pp.

Evidence and Judgment
A Novel
By: Lynn Clarke, J.D.
1-456-50116-X; paperback; 244 pp.

Adventures in Long Island and Abroad
Short Stories
By: Bruce D. Johnson
1-456-54918-9; paperback; 348 pp.

www.anaphoraliterary.wordpress.com
Submissions Welcome: pennsylvaniajournal@gmail.com
Director: Anna Faktorovich

Made in the USA
Lexington, KY
19 August 2011